William J. (William John) Patterson

Harbor dues and transit charges at Montreal and Atlantic ports

William J. (William John) Patterson

Harbor dues and transit charges at Montreal and Atlantic ports

ISBN/EAN: 9783744741538

Printed in Europe, USA, Canada, Australia, Japan

Cover: Foto ©ninafisch / pixelio.de

More available books at **www.hansebooks.com**

Harbor Dues and Transit Charges

AT

Montreal and Atlantic Ports.

———————•••————— ——

A COMMUNICATION FROM THE COUNCIL OF THE
"MONTREAL BOARD OF TRADE," AND THE
COMMITTEE OF MANAGEMENT OF THE
"MONTREAL CORN EXCHANGE ASSOCIATION,"
IN REPLY TO A LETTER FROM

THE

HON. H. L. LANGEVIN, C. B.

MINISTER OF PUBLIC WORKS, OTTAWA,

———————•◆•————————

𝔐𝔬𝔫𝔱𝔯𝔢𝔞𝔩:

D. BENTLEY & CO., PRINTERS.

1880.

HON. H. L. LANGEVIN, C. B.,

MINISTER OF PUBLIC WORKS,

OTTAWA.

SIR,

By instructions from the President of the Board of Trade, and the President of the Corn Exchange Association, I have the honor to transmit the joint reply of their respective Boards, to your letter of 28th June,—in which you were pleased to request answers to certain inquiries relating to Canal Tolls, Harbor Dues, &c. The communication is in four sections, viz.:

1. Statements relating to the Carrying Trade;—on pages 5 to 13 inclusive.

2. Replies in Detail to the Inquiries contained in your letter;—on pages 14 to 31 inclusive.

3. Additional Information;—on pages 32 to 42 inclusive.

4. Summary of Conclusions;—on pages 43 and 44.

It is regretted that so much time has elapsed before this joint answer could be presented; but it seemed to be essential that all particulars in any way bearing upon the subject should be succinctly laid before you, and in doing this, much more time has been occupied than was at first anticipated.

I am now to express to you the hope that the varied information submitted may enable you, in concert with your Colleague, the Minister of Railways and Canals, to present such recommendations to the Government, as will secure the speedy removal of all the burdens and disabilities which prevent the expansion of Canadian Commerce by the River St. Lawrence. If this shall be the result of your deliberations, you will be instrumental in conferring a great boon upon the Mercantile and Shipping interests, as well as upon the general trade of the whole country.

I am only further to suggest that, if you consider it desirable to have a few more copies of the appended document to enable you to furnish one to such of the Cabinet Ministers as may, along with yourself, wish to examine the details submitted,—I am directed by the Presidents to comply with any instruction from you in the matter.

I have the honor to be,

SIR,

Your obedient servant,

WM. J. PATTERSON,

Secretary, Board of Trade, and Corn Exchange Association.

SIR,

I am directed to acknowledge, with the thanks of the Hon. the Minister, the receipt of your letter of the 12th inst., and the accompanying pamphlet, entitled "HARBOR DUES AND TRANSIT CHARGES AT MONTREAL AND ATLANTIC PORTS," being "a Communication from the Council of the Montreal Board of Trade, and the Committee of Management of the Montreal Corn Exchange Association."

In accordance with the suggestion and offer contained in your letter, the Hon. the Minister requests that you will be so kind as to furnish him with fifteen (15) copies of the pamphlet, for the use of his Colleagues.

I have the honor to be,

SIR,

Your obedient servant,

F. H. ENNIS,

Secretary.

WM. J. PATTERSON, Esq.

Secretary Board of Trade,
AND
Corn Exchange Association,

MONTREAL.

INTRODUCTORY.

LETTER FROM THE SECRETARY OF THE BOARD OF TRADE, AND THE CORN EXCHANGE ASSOCIATION.

F. W. HENSHAW, Esq.,

President Board of Trade;

AND

ROBERT ESDAILE, Esq.,

President Corn Exchange Association :—

GENTLEMEN,

Communications were addressed to you respectively, by the Honorable the MINISTER OF PUBLIC WORKS, in which he requested sundry information, that he might " be in a position to fully enter into and discuss the questions recently laid before the Federal Government by the several Deputations from the East and West of Canada,—viz., the freedom, as far as practicable, of the St. Lawrence route." The letters to you were precisely alike. The following is a copy :—

OTTAWA, 28*th June*, 1880.

SIR,

In order to be in a position to fully enter into and discuss the questions recently laid before the Federal Government by the several Deputations from the East and West of Canada, viz. :—the freedom, as far as practicable, of the St. Lawrence route, I am desirous of acquiring certain information which, I believe, the Corn Exchange Association, [the Board of Trade,] and other Public Bodies can furnish me with, the possession of which would enable me, together with my colleague, the Minister of Railways and Canals, to lay before the Privy Council such Report upon the subject as would form the basis of our discussions.

I have therefore the honor to request that you will furnish me with the following Statements :—

1st. A Statement showing the comparative cost of Transport viâ the Erie Canal and the St. Lawrence Canal.

2nd. The Tolls charged on both routes.

3rd. A statement showing the comparative cost of Harbor Dues in Montreal, New York, Philadelphia, Boston and Baltimore.

4th. What reduction in Dues your Board would recommend, either as to Tonnage dues on Vessels, or Wharfage rates on Goods, in order to successfully compete with the Ports above-mentioned ?

5th. The comparative cost of Pilotage at all the above-mentioned Ports, and what remedy your Board would propose in order to reduce the cost of this service below Quebec, as also from Quebec to Montreal.

A

6th. What remedy your Board would propose to lessen the cost of Towage of Sailing Vessels from Father Point to Quebec and from Quebec to Montreal.

I will thank you to let me have the information above-named as soon as practicable, and also to furnish any further data bearing upon this subject.

I remain, Sir,

Your most obedient servant,

HECTOR L. LANGEVIN.

It having been determined that the inquiries could be more satisfactorily made and reported upon jointly, than were your Corporations to submit separate statements, the undersigned was instructed to make investigation and submit proposed answers to the MINISTER's questions; presenting all particulars in the form that may be considered most explicit and useful. This I now have the honor to do; and the only apology that can be made for the delay in presenting my report, is the range of the investigation that seemed necessary, extending over long periods,—and the diversity of particulars which were considered to have a bearing upon the general question.

My aim has mainly been to collect and systematise all available information bearing, directly or indirectly, on matters referred to in the foregoing letter.

This communication has assumed dimensions which, at the outset, were not contemplated. After much condensation, the first section is but little more than a synopsis of the progress of the Carrying Trade of North America during the past quarter of a century. The second, embracing the replies to the Minister's inquiries, is worth examining; and it is hoped that the result of the consideration which the subject is receiving from the mercantile community and the Government, may be the adoption of a policy that will preserve the trade of Canada's Great Water Highway from being broken down, as has been that of the Erie Canal.

The inquiry, of which the matter in the following pages is the out-come, has been a tedious but congenial one; and I have only further to express my solicitude that the particulars adduced may tend to the speedy initiation of measures that will free the inland and ocean commerce of Canada from every obstructive burden.

I am, GENTLEMEN,

Your obedient servant,

WM. J. PATTERSON,

Secretary.

MONTREAL, *6th November*, 1880.

CONTENTS.

———— •>• ————

TRANSPORTATION FROM LAKE ERIE.

The table on page 6 shows the volume of traffic which has been flowing from the level of Lake Erie towards the sea-board during the past twenty-four years,—the quantities of vegetable food of all kinds that were carried eastward by the New York Central and Erie railroads,—the quantities of breadstuffs moved in the same direction via the New York Canals,—the quantities of general eastward traffic by each of these routes,—and the combined aggregates of food and merchandise so transported.

A glance at the last column of that statement will show, in a general way, that the eastward current of traffic during the entire period, has been great, and steadily increasing,—the most notable exceptions being in 1875 and 1876. The railway columns indicate that, for many years by the Erie railway, and since 1869 by the New York Central, much the larger proportions of breadstuffs and general merchandise have passed from the Lake Erie region by these channels; while the Canal traffic, especially in breadstuffs, cannot be said to have been maintained at what it was years ago,—for, since 1861 and 1862, as regards Flour and Wheat, no year's business has equalled either of these. The immense increase in railway traffic to the sea-board through the State of New York, is all the more remarkable when it is remembered that other trunk lines have, for several years, been drawing away freight from the Western and North Western States to ocean ports at Philadelphia and Baltimore. Some idea of the magnitude and growth of the transportation of breadstuffs diverted to these cities, may be formed from the table on page 11.

YEARS.	NEW YORK CENTRAL RAILWAY.		ERIE RAILWAY.		NEW YORK CANALS.		AGGREGATE BY RAILWAYS AND CANALS.	
	Tons of Vegetable Food.	Aggregate Tonnage.	Tons of Vegetable Food.	Aggregate Tonnage.	Tons of Wheat and Flour.	Aggregate Tonnage.	Tons of Food.	Grand Aggregate of Tonnage.
1856...	283,027	776,112	148,943	993,321	475,385	4,116,082	906,355	5,825,415
1857...	275.941	838,791	120,617	978,066	263,141	3,344,061	659,699	5,160,918
1858...	301,507	765,407	154,534	816,965	454,831	3,665,192	910,872	5,237,564
1859...	249,751	834,319	112,727	869,072	250,872	3,781,684	613,350	5,485,075
1860...	343,872	1,028,183	197,233	1,139,554	710,138	4,650,214	1,251,243	6,817,951
1861...	441,562	1,167,302	243,959	1,253,419	1,054,295	4,507,635	1,739,816	6,928,356
1862...	469,885	1,387,433	261,824	1,632,955	1,177,299	5,598,785	1,909,008	8,619,173
1863...	405,380	1,449,604	228,632	1,815,096	846,446	5,557,692	1,480,458	8,822,392
1864...	461,511	1,557,148	215,986	2,170,798	606,891	4,852,941	1,284,388	8,580,887
1865...	349,103	1,275,299	212,677	2,234,350	420,643	4,729,654	982,423	8,239,303
1866...	453,663	1,602,197	397,963	3,242,792	289,166	5,775,220	1,140,792	10,620,209
1867...	495,194	1,667,926	277,432	3,484,546	332,589	5,688,325	1,105,215	10,840,797
1868...	568,680	1,846,599	302,451	3,908,243	390,852	6,442,225	1,261,983	12,197,067
1869...	764,831	2,281,885	322,978	4,312,209	636,670	5,859,080	1,724,479	12,453,174
1870...	1,297,481	4,122,000	468,976	4,852,505	575,684	6,173,769	2,342,141	15,148,274
1871...	1,459,919	4,532,056	745,670	4,844,208	678,450	6,467,888	2,884,039	15,844,152
1872...	1,158,894	4,393,965	711,720	5,564,274	356,917	6,673,370	2,227,531	16,631,609
1873...	1,452,962	5,522,724	584,030	6,312,702	682,827	6,364,782	2,719,819	18,200,208
1874...	1,678,476	6,114,678	791,265	6,364,276	726,702	5,804,588	3,196,443	18,283,542
1875...	1,669,070	6,001,954	674,174	6,239,946	686,709	4,859,958	3,029,953	17,101,858
1876...	2,100,339	6,803,680	775,464	5,972,818	357,683	4,172,129	3,233,486	16,948,627
1877...	1,787,112	6,351,356	706,571	6,182,451	385,072	4,955,963	2,878,755	17,489,770
1878...	2,628,190	7,695,413	1,061,574	6,150,568	811,908	5,171,320	4,507,672	19,017,301
1879...								

The following concise statement shows the eastward and westward traffic earnings of the New York Central and the Erie railways, and the Canals respectively for a period of twenty-four years,—the rates per ton per mile being also given. It appears that, though the rate by canal is 33 to 50 per cent. less than by the railways, the water-route has not been able to hold its own.

YEARS.	N. Y. CENTRAL RAILWAY.		ERIE RAILWAY.		NEW YORK CANALS.	
	Amount of Freight earned.	Average rate per ton per mile.	Amount of Freight earned.	Average rate per ton per mile.	Amount of Freight and Tolls.	Average rate per ton per mile.
1856	$ 4,328,041	2.97 cents.	$ 4,545,782	2.48 cents.	$ 6,573,225	1.11 cents,
1857	4,559,276	3.13 "	4,097,610	2.45 "	3,876,000	7.99 mills.
1858	3,700,270	2.59 "	3,843,310	3 32 "	4,502,437	7.97 "
1859	3,337,148	2.13 "	3,195,869	2.17 "	3,665,806	6.72 "
1860	4,095,934	2.06 "	3,884,343	1.84 "	8,049,450	9.94 "
1861	4,644,449	1.96 "	4,351,464	1.73 "	9,369.378	1.08 cents.
1862	6,607,331	2.22 "	6,642,915	1.89 "	10,780,431	9.59 mills.
1863	7,498,509	2.40 "	8,432,234	2.09 "	9,065,005	8 76 "
1864	8,543,370	2.75 "	9,855,087	2 31 "	10,039,609	1.15 cents.
1865	8,776,028	3.31 "	10,756,264	2.76 "	8,605,961	1.10 "
1866	9,671,920	2.92 "	11,611,023	2.45 "	10,160,051	1.00 "
1867	9,151,750	2.53 "	11,204,689	2 04 "	8,663,119	0.90 "
1868	9,491.427	2.59 "	11,425,739	1.92 "	9,012,659	0.88 "
1869	10,457,582	2.20 "	13,046,804	1.60 "	8,492,131	0 92 "
1870	14,327,418	1.86 "	12,358,027	1.37 "	7,552,988	0 83 "
1871	14,647,580	1.65 "	13,252,235	1.47 "	10,779,887	1.02 "
1872	16,259,647	1.69 "	14,509,745	1.52 "	10,648,711	1.02 "
1873	19,616,018	1.57 "	15,015,808	1.45 "	9,267,503	0.88 "
1874	20,348,735	1.47 "	13,760,042	1.31 "	6,972,607	0.73 "
1875	17,899,702	1.27 "	12,287,400	1.21 "	4,863,137	0.66 "
1876	17,593,265	1.05 "	11,429,930	1.07 "	3,898.919	0.68 "
1877	16,424,316	1.02 "	10,647,807	0.96 "	4,839,033	0.57 "
1878	19,045,830	0.91 "	11,914,489	0.97 "	3,936,520	0.42 "
1879	....	....	....	....	....	....

The foregoing particulars regarding the eastward movement from Lake Erie have been gathered out of the Annual Reports of the Auditor of the New York State Canals.

TRANSPORTATION FROM LAKE ONTARIO.

The following summary statement shows the aggregate of Flour and Grain which passed eastward from the level of Lake Ontario during the past eleven years. The details have appeared from time to time in the Annual Reports of the Trade and Commerce of Montreal :—

	BUSHELS.		BUSHELS.
1869	30,852,440	1875	28,582,150
1870	30,120,551	1876	27,856,724
1871	35,659,298	1877	31,324,811
1872	31,878,595	1878	29,808,195
1873	32,449,369	1879	33,963,698
1874	35,124,651		

The annual average movement appears to have been 31,601,853 bushels. The lowest quantity (in 1876) was 11·85 per cent. below the average; the highest (in 1871) was 12·84 per cent. above it; while the quantity in 1879 was 7·47 per cent. above the average of the period, and only 9·09 per cent. above the quantity in 1869.

The following per centages show that the current of transportation from Lake Ontario to the sea-board does not nearly all flow down the River St. Lawrence :—

	OSWEGO.	CHARLOTTE.	FAIR HAVEN.	CAPE VINCENT	OGDENSBURG.	MONTREAL.
	Per Cent.	Per Cent.	Per Cent.	Per Cent.	Per Cent.	Per Cent.
1869.....	43·42	0·27	....	0.68	13·36	42·27
1870.....	40·77	0.37	....	1·51	15·43	41·92
1871.....	39·64	0.29	....	1·49	13·89	44·69
1872.....	28·83	0·60	....	1·35	14·00	55·22
1873.....	26·34	0·24	....	0·97	11·39	61·06
1874.....	37·02	0·30	....	0·97	11·96	49·75
1875.....	29·48	0·67	....	1·02	8·94	59·89
1876.....	27·57	0·54	....	1·05	3·50	67·54
1877.....	29·23	0·12	0.39	0·74	10·91	58·61
1878.....	17·34	0·20	0.50	0·76	11·20	70·00
1879.....	23·00	0·05	0·73	0·65	9·72	65·85

It appears that the movement via Oswego has diminished considerably,—a good deal of variation has taken place as regards Ogdensburg,—while the figures for Montreal indicate an increase. During five years (1870 to 1874) the annual average for Montreal was 50·53 per cent. of the whole; while during the last half of the decade, the yearly per centage was 64·38.

TRAFFIC MOVEMENT FROM BOTH LAKES.

The preceding statements show separately the movements from Lakes Erie and Ontario, and how small, comparatively speaking, is the traffic of the latter;—a concise view of this transportation question has also been presented in a series of tables by the Commissioner of Inland Revenue, and presented in his Annual Report to the Dominion Government. Mr. Brunel's classification is comprehensive, and the contrasts are made clearly,—confirming, from a different stand-point, the conclusion from figures derived from other sources. The following table is re-formed from his Report :—

	1 New York Canals.	2 Welland Canal.	3 New York Central and Erie Railways.	4 Cleared at Buffalo and Tonawandu.	5 Cleared at Oswego.	6 Via Welland Canal, from U.S. to U.S. Ports.
	Tons.	Tons.	Tons.	Tons.	Tons.	Tons.
1869	1,302,613	503,860	1,087,809	786,436	267,815	337,530
1870 Total	1,295,010	596,749	1,766,457	802,592	238,181	337,384
1870 Inc. or dec.	−0·58	+18·43	+62·36	+2·05	+11·06	+0·04
1871 Total	1,850,198	668,676	2,205,589	1,315,693	297,424	384,585
1871 Inc. or dec.	+42·03	+32·59	+102·75	+67·29	+11·05	+13·94
1872 Total	1,674,320	623,448	1,870,614	1,317,276	169,818	316,619
1872 Inc. or dec.	+28·53	+23·73	+71·96	+67·50	−36·59	−6·19
1873 Total	1,745,171	540,050	2,036,992	1,432,174	131,765	236,743
1873 Inc. or dec.	+33·97	+7·18	+87·25	+82·01	−50·08	−29·86
1874 Total	1,767,598	622,558	2,791,517	1,157,503	243,325	290,114
1874 Inc. or dec.	+35·96	+23·56	+156·62	+47·18	−9·14	−14·04
1875 Total	1,305,550	511,990	2,343,241	1,017,559	126,763	291,473
1875 Inc. or dec.	+0·22	+1·61	+115·04	+29·38	−52·71	−13·55
1876 Total	1,064,293	455,022	2,875,803	783,331	99,975	181,885
1876 Inc. or dec.	−18·29	−9·59	+165·40	−0·39	−62·67	−46·11
1877 Total	1,408,984	406,567	2,493,683	1,223,100	126,899	169,836
1877 Inc. or dec.	+15·07	−19·03	+129·23	+25·52	−52·61	−49·68
1878 Total	1,912,734	438,889	3,695,764	1,644,301	93,149	161,117
1878 Inc. or dec.	+46·83	−12·89	+239·74	+109·08	−65·21	−52·26
1879 Total	1,833,399	422,735	4,353,617	1,565,543	127,168	126,407
1879 Inc. or dec.	+40·74	−16·10	+300·22	+99·07	−52·51	−62·54

In the preceding table for the decade 1870 to 1879 inclusive, all the increases (+) or decreases (—) from year to year relate to the figures for 1869.

1. There were only two years (1870 and 1876) during which the quantities of food-stuffs carried by the New York Canals were less than in 1869, the difference in 1870 not being worth noting;—in each of the other years, with one exception, the increase was large.

2. As regards the movement by Welland Canal, there were increases during the first six years of the period, but diminutions during the last four which averaged 14·40 per cent. for each.

3. The movements eastward by the two great trunk railways in the State of New York, show a very different result. Every one of the ten years shows augmenting traffic; the increase in 1870 was 62·36 per cent., bounding upward year by year, until in 1879 the augmentation was over 300 per cent.

4. The Canal clearances at Buffalo and Tonawanda show large increases, except in 1870 and 1876.

5. The Canal clearances at Oswego, show a constant *minus* (—) difference, except in 1871.

6. Since the first two years of the decade the quantities of breadstuffs passing through the Welland Canal, between U.S. ports, have decreased,—the diminution becoming much larger in the four years 1876 to 1879.

MOVEMENT OF BREADSTUFFS AT THE SEA-BOARD.

The tabular statement on the opposite page shows concisely the total quantities of Breadstuffs received at, and shipped from, the Atlantic sea-board, during ten years,—Flour and Meal being given in bushels :—

		Boston. Bushels.	New York. Bushels.	Philadelphia. Bushels.	Baltimore. Bushels.	New Orleans. Bushels.	Montreal. Bushels.	Totals. Bushels.
1870.... {	Receipts........	13,102,703	69,921,175	15,307,011	13,819,101	15,480,179	13,106,630	140,736,799
	Shipments........		29,455,814				13,601,310	
1871.... {	Receipts........	15,037,943	89,543,673	20,102,425	17,389,443	14,601,922	16,808,108	173,483,514
	Shipments		43,595,502				16,186,484	
1872.... {	Receipts..	17,068,086	90,930,336	24,117,150	20,571,499	15,256,805	18,115,670	186,059,546
	Shipments.		45,901,493				17,522,957	
1873.... {	Receipts ...	17,926,202	92,137,971	24,949,157	19,099,517	13,214,226	19,989,094	187,316,167
	Shipments........	2,145,364	54,278,072	4,807,620	9,049,545	1,433,278	17,912,572	89,626,451
1874.... {	Receipts	18,000,002	107,273,158	24,625,591	24,036,308	12,205,333	17,070,188	204,000,480
	Shipments........	3,186,318	66,088,650	6,671,334	12,555,090	2,394,476	16,739,580	107,635,438
1875.... {	Receipts........	18,321,063	93,895,082	28,195,330	22,048,569	9,669,296	17,324,137	189,453,477
	Shipments........	3,987,959	50,686,401	8,846,515	11,407,489	774,927	15,363,184	91,066,475
1876.... {	Receipts........	22,753,698	95,949,252	35,546,845	35,310,276	9,544,194	19,086,600	218,190,865
	Shipments........	6,043,298	55,500,158	22,016,515	24,761,307	2,145,818	18,167,642	128,634,738
1877.... {	Receipts........	23,215,457	103,313,782	25,727,260	34,590,303	10,025,381	18,825,184	215,697,367
	Shipments........	5,974,621	62,418,317	13,473,965	25,842,450	3,101,232	17,346,678	128,157,263
1878.... {	Receipts........	27,291,781	152,862,170	45,474,650	47,075,240	14,529,304	21,934,170	309,167,315
	Shipments........	12,941,359	107,819,044	29,876,327	39,724,954	7,606,427	20,899,187	218,867,298
1879.... {	Receipts........	32,798,829	163,124,890	47,398,455	66,799,926	14,895,836	23,192,749	348,210,685
	Shipments........	15,774,076	124,350,932	32,310,473	55,629,594	7,065,416	22,755,946	257,886,437
•1880.... {	Receipts	24,821,240	124,879,001	37,253,615	43,974,977	18,311,647	19,137,515	268,377,995
	Shipments	16,243,017	105,608,677	25,621,840	39,832,684	11,753,340	20,309,822	219,369,380

A close examination of the figures in the column for Montreal, will show an increase of receipts in 1879 of 5·74 per cent. over 1878, the latter year indicating 16·51 per cent. over 1877. The increase of shipments in 1879 over 1878 was 17·15 per cent.,—the increase in the latter year over 1877 being 15·61 per cent. Notwithstanding this local increase, the augmented movement along the sea-board shows that there had been a steady relative decrease, for a number of years, until the present season, when there appears, so far, to be a small increase. The table gives the following results :—

			Receipts.		Shipments.	
In 1870,	Montreal's proportions were		9·31 per cent.		.....	
1871,		"	9·69	"	.....	
1872,	"	"	9·73	"	.....	
1873,	"	"	10·67	"	19·98 per cent.	
1874,	"	"	8·63	"	15·55	"
1875,	"	"	9·14	"	16·87	"
1876,	"	"	8·75	"	14·12	"
1877,	"	"	8·72	"	13·53	"
1878,	"	"	7·09	"	9·54	"
1879,	"	"	6·66	"	8·82	"
*1880,	"	"	7·13	"	9·26	"

The figures for 1880, to which an asterisk (*) is prefixed, in the foregoing table, only include the receipts and shipments at the several ports for the first nine months of the year. They are not from official sources; but have been so carefully collated, as to warrant the belief that they afford a fair approximate statement for general comparison. A small increase in the per centages of receipts and shipments is shown. It is believed that had the tenth month's business for all the ports been included in the table on page 11, the per centages for Montreal would have been decreased; because the receipts and shipments during October, at this port, for the past and present years, show the following unfavorable contrast :—

	1879,	1880.	Decrease.
Receipts, bushels............	3,976,126	3,321,402	654,724
Shipments, "	3,671,150	3,230,961	440,189

INFERENCES FROM THE FOREGOING STATEMENTS.

1st. The current of traffic, say, of grain for Great Britain, appears to flow increasingly eastward without regard (1) to distance, and preferring the longest route; (2) this preference being against the cheaper mode of transport by the Welland Canal and River St. Lawrence; and (3) a fair inference is, (as shown on p. 7,) that railway transport is now much less expensive than it was twenty or thirty years ago. To enable carriers by water, therefore, to maintain a fair relative position, every impediment must be removed, and every item of expense reduced.

2nd. The information tabulated in one of the statements (p. 7) shows, that the great reductions in Canal freights and tolls, from time to time, during the past quarter of a century, have not sufficed to increase, or even to maintain the volume of traffic by the water route.

3rd. The re-imposition of full rates of toll upon merchandise passing through the Canadian Canals in 1863,—(that is to say, the Order-in-Council dated 19th May, 1860, which provided for a refund of 90 per cent. of the tolls in certain cases, at Port Colborne, was rescinded before the opening of navigation in 1863,)—did not lead, for instance, to an increase in the average rate of freight on Wheat from Chicago to Montreal,—reductions being made *pari passu* both by the Welland and the Erie.

4th. The opinion is entertained in Toledo, that the " cheapest route from " thence to Liverpool, via Montreal, has additional advantages over the extra " charges in Buffalo and New York for transfer, and is a great protection to " western shippers." When the enlargement of the Welland Canal is finished, and the removal or reduction of all encumbering tolls and charges is accomplished, the advantages referred to may be realized. Meantime, that opinion seems to be practically confined to those who give expression to it,—as may be inferred from the table and remarks on pp. 9, 10.

5th. Whatever means may be adopted with a view to increase the export and import trade of the Dominion via the River St. Lawrence, it would seem scarcely worth while to consider what effect, if any, would be produced by that action upon east-bound freight from the Western States, other than that in which Canadians may have a direct interest.

6th. The railway from Fort William, on Lake Superior, to Winnipeg and Selkirk,—as well as 150 miles of the main line of the Canada Pacific, to the westward of the latter point,—will be completed before Autumn, 1881, and there is no good reason to doubt that the surplus grain-crop of Manitoba will find its way by railway and the lakes, via the Welland Canal and the River St. Lawrence to Montreal,—if not driven away by high rates of freight and other charges. This alone ought to be sufficient incentive to endeavor to lessen or entirely remove all the rates and dues that can be so dealt with.

REPLIES TO THE INQUIRIES OF THE MINISTER OF PUBLIC WORKS.

I. AND II.—RATES OF FREIGHT AND CANAL TOLLS.

1st. A Statement showing the comparative cost of transport via the Erie Canal and the St. Lawrence Canals.

2nd. The Tolls charged on both routes.

Years.	Chicago to New York, Via Buffalo.				Chicago to New York. Via Oswego.			Chicago to Montreal, by Schooner to Kingston. Through rates.	
	No. of days in Canal.	Highest rate Chicago to Buffalo.	Highest rate Buffalo to New York.	Average rate of Freight.	Highest rate Chicago to Oswego.	Highest rate Oswego to New York.	Average rate of Freight.		Rates by Propellers are variable, according to the state of trade,—sometimes higher than by schooner to Kingston, and sometimes lower.—On the average there is probably no difference.
		Cts.	Cts.	Cts.	Cts.	Cts.	Cts.	Cts.	
1861	$8\frac{1}{2}$	26	30	$27\frac{1}{8}$	$30\frac{1}{2}$	22	27	....	
1862	$8\frac{1}{2}$	17	$24\frac{1}{2}$	$26\frac{1}{4}$	$22\frac{1}{4}$	18	$26\frac{1}{4}$	26	
1863	9	$12\frac{1}{2}$	25	23	17	18	$22\frac{3}{4}$	16	
1864	10	18	22	$28\frac{1}{4}$	24	18	$28\frac{1}{2}$	$18\frac{1}{2}$	
1865	10	19	26	$26\frac{3}{4}$	27	18	$27\frac{1}{4}$	$18\frac{1}{2}$	
1866	10	23	23	$30\frac{1}{2}$	20	20	$31\frac{1}{4}$	$18\frac{1}{2}$	
1867	10	15	25	$22\frac{1}{2}$	$18\frac{1}{2}$	17	$22\frac{1}{2}$	$17\frac{1}{2}$	
1868	10	$13\frac{1}{2}$	24	23	16	17	23	$17\frac{1}{2}$	
1869	10	12	25	23	$16\frac{3}{4}$	20	$23\frac{1}{4}$	16	
1870	10	10	16	17	15	12	$18\frac{3}{4}$	16	
1871	11	18	17	$20\frac{3}{4}$	20	14	$21\frac{1}{4}$	$14\frac{1}{2}$	
1872	11	18	17	$24\frac{1}{4}$	20	14	$23\frac{1}{4}$	$21\frac{1}{4}$	
1873	11	13	13	19	20	9	22	$18\frac{1}{2}$	
1874	11	$6\frac{1}{2}$	$11\frac{1}{2}$	14	$11\frac{1}{2}$	$7\frac{1}{4}$	15	$12\frac{1}{2}$	
1875	11	$6\frac{1}{2}$	11	$11\frac{1}{2}$	10	$9\frac{1}{4}$	$12\frac{3}{4}$	11	
1876	11	5	10	$9\frac{3}{4}$	$7\frac{1}{2}$	9	$11\frac{1}{2}$	10	
1877	11	6	12	11	10	13	$13\frac{1}{4}$	10	
1878	10	$5\frac{1}{4}$	$8\frac{1}{2}$	9	$8\frac{1}{2}$	$7\frac{1}{2}$	13	$8\frac{1}{2}$	
1879	....	....	....	....	....	....	....	8	

The foregoing table shows the average of the rates of freight in each year since 1861; (1.) from Chicago to New York via Buffalo and Erie Canal; (2.) from Chicago to New York via Oswego; and (3.) from Chicago to Montreal via Kingston. The columns showing highest rates by the U. S. water routes are worthy of examination,—especially during the earlier years of the period; while the average rates by the three routes, has been largely in favor of that via the River St. Lawrence, until within the past few years. It scarcely needs to be stated, however, that, while *average* rates for periods of years are *convenient* criteria, they do not always afford sufficient data for conclusions regarding particular seasons. It would be impossible to go into more detail here, however. The average time of the trip of a grain-laden propeller from Chicago to Montreal is less than is occupied by a loaded canal boat in passing through the Erie Canal.

The rates of freight averaged in the table on p. 14 include the Canal Tolls, —transfer charges at Kingston being also included in the rates to Montreal. The full toll per ton of 2000 lbs., on Wheat, passing down the Welland Canal, is 20c., or say ⅝c. per bushel of 60 lbs. When this rate is paid, the cargo is entitled to pass *free* through the St. Lawrence Canals. This has been the tariff rate for more than twenty years,—except when by Order-in-Council, of 19th May, 1860, a refund of 90 per cent., in certain cases, was directed to be made at Port Colborne, and free traffic was provided for on the St. Lawrence Canals. The Order-in-Council was revoked in 1863, as stated on p. 13.

The rates by the Erie Canal on a bushel of wheat transported from Buffalo to Troy, in each season of navigation during nineteen years, were as follows :—

	FREIGHT AND TOLLS.			TOLLS ALONE WERE.				FREIGHT AND TOLLS.			TOLLS ALONE WERE.		
	c.	m.	f.	c.	m.	f.		cf	m.	f.	c.	m.	f.
1861......	15	7	5	5	1	7	1871......	12	6	2	3	1	0
1862......	15	8	4	6	2	1	1872......	13	1	0	3	1	0
1863......	15	3	9	6	2	1	1873......	11	5	7	3	1	0
1864......	18	7	8	6	2	1	1874......	10	1	1	3	1	0
1865......	16	8	4	6	2	1	1875......	8	0	1	2	0	7
1866......	16	9	6	6	2	1	1876......	6	7	1	2	0	7
1867......	15	6	9	6	2	1	1877......	7	3	9	1	0	3
1868......	15	6	5	6	2	1	1878......	5	9	9	1	0	3
1869......	16	3	1	6	2	1	1879......	....			1	0	3
1870......	11	2	2	3	1	0	1880......	....			1	0	3

No tolls are levied on any of the following articles when transported on the New York Canals :—

*Pork.	*Wool.	Hops.
*Beef.	*Live Cattle, Hogs, and Sheep	Domestic Spirits.
*Bacon.	Cotton.	Oil Cake.
*Cheese.	Tobacco, unmanufactured.	Bar and Pig Lead.
*Butter.	Hemp.	Domestic Woollens.
*Lard.	Clover and Grass Seed.	" Cottons.
*Tallow.	Flax Seed.	Coffee.

The rate of toll that would be levied on the articles to which an asterisk (*) is prefixed, on passing *each way* through the Welland Canal, is 20c. per ton ; the rate upon the others is 40c. per ton.

———————

III.—HARBOR DUES AND OTHER CHARGES.

3rd. A Statement showing the comparative cost of Harbor Dues in Montreal, New York, Philadelphia, Boston and Baltimore.

It may be stated here, that the Council of the Board of Trade had the questions of Pilotage, Towage, and Harbor Charges, under consideration more than a year ago; and a report was made which contained an *approximate* comparative statement of charges to a vessel of 600 tons register, drawing 18 feet water, inwards and outwards, as follows :

	PILOTAGE.	TOWAGE.	WHARFAGE.
Boston	$86.37	$60	......
New York	172 80	100	$6 per day and fee of $9.
Philadelphia	162.00	120	$3 per day.
Baltimore	162.00	150	$1 per day.
Montreal	193.50	$450 @ $600	$4.50 per day.

Foreign ships pay a yearly tax of 30c. per ton register in the United States ports.

This general statement was necessarily partial, for the column of " Wharfage " does not include ordinary charges to which all vessels are liable, owing to the difficulty that was experienced in obtaining details. The particulars given on pp. 17 to 23 inclusive, admit of very much fuller and specific comparisons.

As supplementary to the taxes and dues levied at the ports referred to by the MINISTER OF PUBLIC WORKS the subjoined list shows the various items of charge exacted by the Federal Government upon all vessels engaged in the foreign trade on entering or leaving United States ports,—as provided for by the Customs and Navigation Laws.

U. S. CHARGES ON VESSELS INWARD.

Tonnage duties on Vessels, in the foreign trade, built in the U. S., per ton register	$ .30
Tonnage duties on Foreign Vessels, per ton register	.50
Tonnage tax (besides the duty, in certain cases,) per ton register	.30
Light-money, per ton register	.50
Entry fee at Custom House, when cargo is free goods	2.50
" " " when cargo contains dutiable goods	5.50
General Order	.20
Each Jurat	.20
Permits. To land Chronometer, Sails, &c.	.20
United States Hospital Money. Charged on American Vessels for each employé on board for their time of service since date of last entry of Vessel in a U. S. port,—per month	.30
Post Entry	2.00
U. S. Commissioner's fees for paying crew, per man	.50

U. S. CHARGES ON VESSELS OUTWARD.

U. S. Commissioner's fees for shipping crew, per man	$2.00
Charge for log-book and papers	3.00
Clearance from Custom House	2.50
Bill of Health	.20
Crew Bond	.40
Crew List certified	.25
Shipping Articles	.20

A communication recently received from the Assistant-Secretary of the Treasury of the United States, affords the following particulars from the Navigation Laws, on the subject of "Tonnage Duties," which are worth recording here :—

SEC. 4219.--Upon vessels which shall be entered in the United States from any foreign port or place there shall be paid duties as follows :—

(a.) On vessels built within the United States but belonging wholly or in part to subjects of foreign powers, at the rate of thirty cents per ton.

(b.) On other vessels not of the United States, at the rate of fifty cents per ton.

(c.) Upon every vessel not of the United States, which shall be entered in one district from another district, having on board goods, wares, or merchandise taken in one district to be delivered in another district, duties shall be paid at the rate of fifty cents per ton. Nothing in this section shall be deemed in anywise to impair any rights or privileges which have been or may be acquired by any foreign nation under the laws and treaties of the United States relative to the duty of tonnage on vessels.

(*d.*) On all foreign vessels which shall be entered in the United States from any foreign port or place, to and with which vessels of the United States are not ordinarily permitted to enter and trade, there shall be paid a duty at the rate of two dollars per ton ; and none of the duties on tonnage above-mentioned shall be levied on the vessels of any foreign nation if the President of the United States shall be satisfied that the discriminating or countervailing duties of such foreign nations, so far as they operate to the disadvantage of the United States have been abolished.

(*e.*) In addition to the tonnage-duty above imposed, there shall be paid a tax, at the rate of thirty cents per ton, on vessels which shall be entered at any custom-house within the United States from any foreign port or place ; and any rights or privileges acquired by any foreign nation under the laws and treaties of the United States relative to the duty of tonnage on vessels shall not be impaired.

(*f.*) And any vessel, any officer of which shall not be a citizen of the United States shall pay a tax of fifty cents per ton.   (See § 4131.)

SEC. 4220.—No vessel belonging to any citizen of the United States, trading from one port within the United States to another port within the United States, or employed in the bank, whale, or other fisheries, shall be subject to tonnage tax or duty, if such vessel be licensed, registered or enrolled.

SEC. 4221.—In cases of vessels making regular daily trips between any port of the United States and any port in the Dominion of Canada, wholly upon interior waters not navigable to the ocean, no tonnage or clearance fees shall be charged against such vessel by the officers of the United States, except upon the first clearing of such vessel in each year.

SEC. 2793.—Enrolled or licensed vessels engaged in the foreign and coasting trade on the northern, northeastern and northwestern frontiers of the United States, departing from or arriving at a port in one district to or from a port in another district, and also touching at intermediate foreign ports shall not thereby become liable to the payment of entry and clearance fees, or tonnage tax, as if from or to foreign ports : but such vessels shall, notwithstanding, be required to enter and clear.

SEC. 4223.—The tonnage duty imposed on all vessels engaged in foreign commerce shall be levied but once within one year, and, when paid by such vessel, no further tonnage tax shall be collected within one year from the date of such payment.   But this provision shall not extend to foreign vessels entered in the United States from any foreign port, to and with which vessels of the United States are not ordinarily permitted to enter and trade.

SEC. 4224.—Vessels within pay tonnage duties once in a year, shall pay the same either at their first clearance from or entry at, according to priority, a custom-house in the United States in each calendar year. Nothing in this section shall be construed to prevent customs officers from collecting such tonnage duty at the entry of vessels at their respective custom-houses during the calendar year if the same has not previously been paid for such year.

SEC. 4225.—A duty of fifty cents per ton, to be denominated " light-money," shall be levied and collected on all vessels not of the United States, which may enter the ports of the United States.   Such light-money shall be levied and collected in the same manner and under the same regulations as the tonnage duties.

SEC. 4226.—The preceding section shall not be deemed to operate upon unregistered vessels, owned by citizens of the United States, and carrying a sea-letter, or other regular document, issued from a custom-house of the United States, proving the vessel to be American property.

Vesssels entering from a foreign port or place.—I. All merchant-vessels entered in the United States from any foreign port or place, are subject to the payment of tonnage duty.   They may be divided into two principal classes, namely :—Vessels of the United States, and vessels not of the United States.   Vessels of the United States are those documented according to law.   They pay 30 cents per ton under paragraph *e*, § 4219, except those any of whose officers are not citizens of the United States, which pay 50 cents per ton under paragraph *f.*   The officers of a vessel are, under the rulings of the Department, the master and mates, and, in addition, the engineers and pilots, if a steam-vessel.

II.—Vessels not of the United States may be divided, in relation to the rates of tonnage duty, into five classes :

1. Vessels built in the United States, but belonging wholly or in part to subjects of foreign powers.

2. Vessels not built in the United States, and belonging wholly or in part to subjects of foreign powers.

3. Vessels wherever built, owned in whole or in part by subjects of foreign powers, which enter from a foreign place where vessels of the United States are not ordinarily permitted to enter and trade.

4. Vessels not built in the United States, but belonging to citizens of the United States, and provided only with a sea-letter, or other custom-house document proving the vessel to be American property.

5. Vessels without documents.

III.—Vessels of class 1 pay 30 cents per ton under paragraph *a*, § 4219, 30 cents per ton additional under paragraph *e*, and 50 cents per ton " light-money" under § 4225, making $1.10 in all.

Vessels of class 2 pay 50 cents per ton under paragraph *b*, 30 cents per ton additional under paragraph *e*, and 50 cents per ton " light-money" under § 4225, making $1.30 in all.

Vessels of class 3 pay $2 per ton under paragraph *d*, 30 cents per ton additional under paragraph *e*, and 50 cents per ton " light-money " under § 4225, making $2.80 in all.

Vessels of class 4 pay 50 cents per ton under paragraph *b*, and 30 cents per ton additional under paragraph *e*, making 80 cents per ton ; and if the owner or master refuses to take the oath required by § 4226, 50 cents per ton " light-money " under § 4225 must be paid, making $1.30 per ton.

Vessels of class 5 pay the same as vessels of class 1 or 2, accordingly as they are vessels built in the United States or not.   The collector must satisfy himself, by evidence presented, that the vessel was built in the United States, before admitting her to payment under class 1 at $1.10 per ton.   (No importations can be permitted in vessels of class 5.   See § 2597, Rev. Stat.)

1.—Port of Boston.

The following are the rates and dues levied on sea-going vessels at this port :—

Customs Entry—100 tons and over, dutiable cargo..............$5.50
          "   "   free cargo.................. 3.17
Custom Clearance—under license............................. 0.50
            under register 1.50
            foreign vessel coastwise.... .... 2.00
            "   foreign.................... 3.30

☞ *With reference to the foregoing particulars from local sources, see the list of U. S. Government charges upon foreign vessels, as well as upon American vessels in the foreign trade, on pages* 17, 18.

Wharfage, Dockage—Vessels discharging cargo, or loading grain at elevators, or other cargoes at the wharves, are free from wharfage.

            Steamers, 1c. per day per ton register.

            Sailing vessels over 200 tons register ½c. per ton per day.

Lay-Days free from Dockage as follows :—

Loading.		*Discharging.*	
200 to 500 tons.............20 days.		200 to 500 tons.............. 7 days.	
500 to 800 " ....25 "		500 to 800 " ....10 "	
800 to 1100 " ....35 "		800 to 1100 " ....15 "	
1100 to 1500 " ....40 "		1100 to 1500 " ....20 "	
Over 1500 " ....45 "		Over 1500 " ....25 "	

Note—The foregoing information is from an "*Index to the Port of Boston.*" Some explanations and further information have been received from a reliable source as follows :—

Wharfage.—No charge for wharfage is made to the vessel ;—the shipper or receiver pays it. When a vessel goes to a railroad dock to discharge, the wharfage is free on that portion of the cargo which goes over the road ;—and the same rule applies to a vessel loading at a railroad dock ; that portion of her cargo which comes over the road is free from wharfage. In all cases where cargo is received from, or delivered to lighter or other vessel over side, while the vessel is at a wharf, the goods so received or delivered are subject to half-wharfage.

Particular Rates.—When the goods do not come over a railroad, to its dock where the vessel is loading, the charges on principal articles are as follows :—

Flour per brl..............4c.		Butter, per tub............. 1c.	
" per sack ....2c.		Hay, per ton............ ......40c.	
Cheese, per box ....1c.		Cattle Feed per bag........ 2c.	
Lard, per tierce............7c.		Cattle, per head ....15c.	
Bacon, per box ....6¼c.		Sheep or Hogs, per head.... 4c.	

N. B.—Cattle, sheep, and Live Stock, are invariably subject to wharfage, whether coming over the railway or not.

Grain-Transfer and other Charges.

Grain in bulk, delivered by floating elevator, ¾c. to 1¼c. per bushel.
 "   "   loading and trimming, per 1000 bush...... $1.50 to $2.
Hire of bags (to be returned to port,) each.............. .05
Stowing and sewing bags, each........................ .01½
Ceiling (Lining) for cargo, 1¼c. per bush.;—should serve
 for 3, 4, or 5 voyages.
Surveyor's Fee.......................................$10.00

2.—PORT OF NEW YORK.

The following rates and dues are paid by all sea-going vessels :—

Quarantine Dues....................................$6.50
Hospital Dues—for Captain........................... 1.50
 for each Mate........................... 1.00
 for each Seaman........................ 50
Health Officer...................................... 6.50

With reference to the foregoing particulars from local sources, see the list of U.S. Government charges upon foreign vessels, as well as upon American vessels in the foreign trade, on pages 17, 18.

Wharfage—All vessels of 200 tons and under, per ton.... 2c. per day.
 All vessels over 200 tons, 2c. per day for each of the first
 200 tons ; and for each additional ton ½c. per day.
The owner, or lessee of a wharf may charge 5c. per ton per day, for all
 merchandise left on his wharf, after 24 hours have elapsed from
 the time of being landed or left there.
Harbor Master's Fee, from $3 to $24, according to size of vessel,—the
 legal charge being 1½c. per ton.

Ballast—discharging.............................. 35c. per ton.
 Loading, stone, f. o. b...................... 60c.   "
 "   shingle, f. o. b..................... 65c.   "
 "   earth, f. o. b...................... 50c.   "

Grain-Transfer and other Charges.

Elevating—into single-deck vessels, including trimming, p. 1000 bu. $7.00
 into double-deck vessels, including trimming, p. 1000 bu. 8.00
Delivering in bags on ocean vessels, per 1000 bushels 6.25
 "   "   coastwise vessels including trimming...... 2.50
Loading bags, per 1000 bushels............................. 5.00
Hire of bags (to be returned to port,) per 100 bags.............. 4.00
Ceiling (Lining) for Grain in bulk, per 100 bushels.............. 75

3.—PORT OF PHILADELPHIA.

The charges paid by all sea-going vessels are as follows:—

Entrance Fee............$2.50 | Clearance Fee...........$2.50
Harbor Master........... 2.00 | Bill of Health........... .20
Surveyor's Fee........... 3.00 | Certified Manifest........ .20
Manifest Stamp........$1 to $2 |

With reference to the foregoing particulars from local sources, see the list of U.S. Government charges upon foreign vessels, as well as upon American vessels in the foreign trade, on pages 17, 18.

Wharfage Dues on a Ship............................$4.00 per day.
     "   on a Barque, Brig, or Schooner ...... 3.00   "

While, in a general way, these rates are correct, the following items are more specific :—Charges at the city wharves, from $2 to $5 per day ; at the oil piers, $3.50 per day for vessels under 300 tons ; $4.50 on vessels between 300 and 500 tons ; $5.50 on vessels between 500 and 800 tons ; $6.50 on vessels between 800 and 1000 tons ; and $7 for vessels of over 1000 tons. Rates at grain-loading wharves do not exceed $2 per day,—at some wharves *free*.

Spanish, Portuguese, Italian, Russian, and South American Ships pay a sum of $2.50 in addition to charges for Pilotage.

Stone ballast—$1.00 to $1.50 per ton.

Grain-Transfer and other Charges.

Loading Grain in bulk, per 1000 bushels $2.40
     "   in bags,   " 5.60
Hire of bags, (to be returned to port,) per 100 bags 3.00
Ceiling (Lining) for bulk grain, ¾c. to 1c. per bushel.
Surveyor's Fee 10.00

4.—Port of Baltimore.

The following rates are levied on all sea-going vessels :—

Vessels with dutiable cargo pay as follows :—

          Customs Entry..................$2.50
              "   Survey................... 3.00
              "   Permits .... .20

Vessels with duty-free cargo pay :—

          Customs Entry..................$2.50
              "   Survey................. .67

☞ *With reference to the foregoing particulars from local sources, see the list of U.S. Government charges upon foreign vessels, as well as upon American vessels in the foreign trade, on pages 17, 18.*

Quarantine and Doctor's fees—1c. per ton register.

Wharfage per day :—Vessels of less than 400 tons..............$1.25
                              400 to 600 tons........ 1.50
                              600 to 800 tons........ 1.75
                              800 tons and upwards.. 2.00

These rates apply to wharves owned or leased by individuals, where cargoes of all descriptions are landed and shipped. At wharves owned by the City or State, the rate is 1c. per ton register per day ; at the grain-elevator, $1.50 per day for vessels up to 500 tons register, and $2 if larger ; at oil-wharves, $3.50 per day on all vessels irrespective of size.

Ballast :—Discharging, per ton,........................... 20c. to 30c.
          Loading and cost of earth or stone, per ton...... 50c. to 70c.

Grain-Transfer and other Charges.

Elevating bulk grain, per 100 bushels...................... 38c.

Trimming   "   per 1000 bushels...................... $1.50

Stowing bags, per 1000 bushels........................... .05

Bag-hire (bags to be returned to port,) per 100 .... 3.00

Sewing bags, per 100..................................... .50

Ceiling (Lining) for Grain in bulk, 1½c. per bushel ; the same lining, with slight repairs, should serve for 4 or 5 voyages.

Surveyor's Fee 10.00

5.—PORT OF MONTREAL.

The following dues and charges are levied on all sea-going craft :—

Hospital Dues.....................2c. per ton register.

* Police Dues......................3c.   "

Wharf Dues—Steamships, of 50 tons register, and upwards, per day..............1½c. per ton register.

"   Sailing Vessels, of 50 tons register, and upwards, per day............ ¾c.   "

The Harbor Commissioners are authorized by an Order-in-Council, dated 19th April, 1880 to levy rates upon "all merchandise, animals, and things whatsoever, landed or shipped in the harbor." The printed tariff contains an enumeration of nearly 300 items, to which specified rates are attached. The charges on two-thirds of these are at the rate of 20c. to 50c. per ton, viz. :—on 13 items, 20c. per ton; on 38 items, 25c. per ton ; ou 80 items, 30c. per ton ; on 28 items, 40c. per ton ; and on 19 items, 50c. per ton.

Wheat, Maize, Peas, Barley, Malt, are charged 25c. per 100 bushels; and Oats 15c. per 100 bushels.

It is also provided :—" On all goods, wares, and merchandise whatsoever, " the quantity of which by weight, measurement, or other mode " of estimate provided for in the tariff, cannot be conveniently " ascertained, it shall be lawful for the Harbor Commissioners to " levy a rate of ¼ of 1 per cent. on the value thereof."

Grain-Transfer and other Charges, 1880.

The Harbor Commissioners levy the following rates (as above-noted) :—

Upon Wheat, Indian Corn, Barley, Malt, Peas, &c., per 100 bushels............................. 25c.

"   Oats, per 100 bushels,........................ 15c.

---

* Trinity Dues—5 p.ct. on all Pilotage—is a charge deducted from the pilotage accounts, and is understood to go into the Fund for Decayed Pilots.

Transfer rates by floating elevators are :—

Elevating, (one-half of which is payable by the receiving
vessel) per bush........ .... ⅓c.

Filling and sewing Grain-bags, each bag .... ¾c. to 1c.

Hire of Grain-bags, including filling and sewing (to be
returned to port,) per bag .... 4½c.

Through cargoes of grain by railway from the West for shipment at
Montreal for Europe, are transferred from the cars, floated to
vessel in harbor, and put f. o. b., for a charge of 1¾c. per bu. for
all local expenses, which charge is usually included in the
through-freight rate.—Free storage for a term of 10 days is also
granted when required.

Storage of Grain cargoes—¼c. per bu. for first five days.

⅛c. per bu. for each of next three terms of five
days each respectively.

⅛c. per bu. for each succeeding term of 10
days.

Winter rate for the season (Nov. 1 to May 15)
2½ c. per bu.

Charges for Lining (Ceiling) for Grain-cargoes :—

Wooden Ships, per register ton,.... ....45 to 60c.

Iron Ships, which are not lined higher than the turn of
the bilge, per ton ... . ,..... ....30 to 40c.

The same lining, with occasional slight repairs. should
serve for three or four voyages.

Steamers with water-ballast tanks, when tank covers are
clear, dry and caulked, require no lining

Port Warden's Fee.............. .... $4 to $6

Special Rates and Charges, 1880.

Harbor Towages—For one tug......... .... $5 @ $10

For two tugs........................ .... $20

Ballast—Wharfage on................................ 10c. per ton

Carting away ... . 20c. "

Laid down alongside, when required .... 50c. "

Tallyman, when required,................ .... $2.00 per day of 10 hours.

Watchman, " .... $2.00 for 12 hours.

Customs Officer—overtime when discharging, $2.50 per night.

Shipping-Master's Fee for British Vessels, for
each man shipped or discharged..... 50 cents.

Noting Protest, $1.00 ;—Extending Protest, when required, $5.00.

Stevedore's charges for discharging inwards, and loading outwards
cargoes, are from 16c. to 20c. per ton, for both weight and
measurement.

IV.—REPEAL AND REDUCTION OF HARBOR DUES.

4th. What reduction in Dues your Board would recommend, either as to Tonnage Dues on Vessels, or Wharfage rates on Goods, in order to successfully compete with the Ports above-mentioned?

1. Through rates of freight for merchandise, for instance, from Great Britain to Toronto and other points in Ontario, are practically the same, whether the ocean carriage terminates at New York, Boston, or Montreal. There are no wharfage rates imposed at either of the two former ports, on merchandise in transit for inland points either in the U.S. or Canada. Wharfage rates at Montreal, however, are a considerable item. Taking the keenness of competition in every department of mercantile life into account, it is thought that an effectual remedy would be, *to have all these rates promptly repealed*, for they weigh heavily on the foreign commerce of the Dominion, and send freight past Canadian ships and steamers into round-about foreign channels, to find cheaper access to cities and towns in Ontario.

2. The following statement shows the operation of the tariff which the Montreal Harbor Commissioners were, in April last, authorized to enforce (see page 22;) and it demonstrates the necessity for reducing the dues :—

		1878	1879	1880 To 1st October.
Sea-going traffic :				
Wharfage dues on	Imports...........	$59,216	$84,207	$91,200
do.	Exports		67,644	57,500
do.	Steamships	103,046	41,975	54,800
do.	Sailing Vessels...		16,442	
		$162,262	$210,268	$203,500
Local traffic :				
Wharfage dues on	Goods.............	$8,190	$6,648	
do.	Barges............	18,497	17,625	$30,514
do.	Steamboats, &c.....	25,473	22,891	
		$52,160	$47,164	$30,514
		162,262	210,268	203,500
Yearly Totals......		$214,422	$257,432	$234,014

The harbor revenue in 1879 amounted to $269,596 ;—the dues levied on imported and exported merchandise, appear to have been 56·52 per cent. of that income. If the dues on the steamships and sailing vessels carrying the goods were added, the burden imposed would be about 66 per cent. The effect would simply be, the addition of about $180,000 to the cost of the property carried to and from the port of Montreal,— which would have been saved in the ports of Boston, New York, Philadelphia and Baltimore.

3. The subjoined statement shows how wharfage charges affect steamships and sailing vessels in the several Atlantic Ports, as compared with Montreal, according to the rates cited on pages 19, 20, 21 and 22,—the example being that of a 1,500-ton vessel:—

		Steamships.	Sailing Vessels.
* Boston...... per day		$15.00	$ 7.50
New York... do.		10.50	10.50
Philadelphia, do.		4.00	4.00
† Baltimore... do.		2.00	2.00
Montreal.... do.		22.50	11.25

4. It is understood that, during the past ten years, the revenue from foreign traffic averaged 74·37 per cent. of the total revenue,—the expenditure on harbor-works in ten years being about $80,000 less than was spent in seven years upon works in the river. The amount paid as interest on the Government loan in four years was not much under $200,000, and on the Harbor debt in ten years $840,000. The revenue, in ten years, from wharfage dues on sea-going vessels was $1,738,600;—if the Harbor Trust were immediately relieved by Government, and by the City of Montreal, from debt obligations, an immense reduction (say 75 per cent.) in wharfage dues might signalize the opening of navigation in 1881.

5. It will be observed that this suggested reduction does not affect revenue from local sources; such would very likely be increased by the influx of sea-going vessels. In that case, the Harbor Trust could give attention to other reductions and economies, *which would soon make Montreal the cheapest port in the world for the sea-going craft of all nations.*

V.—RATES OF PILOTAGE.

5th The Comparative cost of Pilotage at all the above mentioned Ports, and what remedy your Board would propose in order to reduce the cost of this service below Quebec, as also from Quebec to Montreal.

1.—PORT OF BOSTON.

The rates for piloting a 600-ton sailing vessel, drawing 18 feet water, from Boston Light (distance 9 miles from Boston proper) are :—

Inward, $3.80 per foot draft,.. $68.40
Outward, $2.75   "   " 49.50

$117.90

* For some exceptions to the rule in Boston harbor, see page 19, under the word "Wharfage."
† For exceptions, see paragraph near the foot of page 21.

Pilotage is practically compulsory, both for steam and sail vessels ;—they generally lay-to and wait for a Pilot, rather than incur risk without one. If a vessel is boarded 15, 20 or even 25 miles outside of Boston Light, in summer, (say April to November,) the Pilot is entitled to no more than if he had been taken within 100 yards of it. In winter he is entitled to distance-money, but must go on board four miles beyond Minot's Light, which is 9 miles further out than Boston Light,—the total distance being 22 miles. The distance-money for 18 feet draft would be $13.68, making the winter rate $131.58.

All U.S. vessels, regardless of size, are exempted from the necessity to engage a Pilot when under coasting license. Vessels under 200 tons register, when sailing under a register, may decline the services of a Pilot, and pay half pilotage.

2.—PORT OF NEW YORK.

The charges for piloting a 600-ton sailing vessel drawing 18 feet water from Sandy-Hook to New York (a distance of 21 miles) are :—

Inward, $5.50 per foot draft,............................	$99.00
Outward, $4.10 " "	73.80
	$172.80

The distance from the Battery, (the southern point of the city,) to the bar, and over it, at Sandy-Hook, is 21 miles. When the wind is fair, Pilots usually leave the vessel when well over the bar; if the wind is ahead, they take the vessel to the light-ship, which is 6 miles farther.

The sum of $4, is added to the rates inward and outward respectively, between 1st November and 1st April.

Pilotage is compulsory for all foreign vessels; but the Act regulating the service provides that "no master of a vessel belonging to a citizen of the United States, and "licensed and employed in the carrying trade by way of Sandy-Hook, shall be required "to employ a licensed Pilot."

3.—PORT OF PHILADELPHIA.

The cost of pilotage from Philadelphia to the Capes of the Delaware (103 miles) for a 600-ton sailing vessel drawing 18 feet water, would be :—

Inward, $4.50 per foot draft............................	$81.00
Outward, same rate, ...	81.00
	$162.00

Pilotage is compulsory for all vessels arriving from, or bound to, a foreign port.
Spanish, Portuguese, Italian, Russian, and South American ships have to pay $2.50 in addition to the usual cost of pilotage.

4.—PORT OF BALTIMORE.

The pilotage distance to Cape Henry is 177 miles. The charges to a 600-ton sailing vessel, drawing 18 feet water, are:—

Inward, $5 per foot draft,...	$90.00
Outward, same rate, ...	90.00
	$180.00

If a vessel is hailed outside the limit at the Cape, she must take a Pilot; but if inside on being hailed, it is optional with the master to do so or not.

Coasting vessels pay a yearly tax of 6c. per ton, and are exempt from pilotage.

5.—PORT OF MONTREAL.

The pilotage charges to a 600-ton sailing vessel, drawing 18 feet water, when towed, are as follows:—

Father Point to Quebec, 161 miles,—$3.60 per foot....	$64.80	
Quebec to Father Point,—$3.15 per foot,.............	56.70	
		$121.50
Quebec to Montreal, 150 miles, $2 per foot,.............	$36.00	
Montreal to Quebec, same rate	36.00	
		72.00
		$193.50

It should be stated, that, from 10th to 19th of November, the rates from Father Point or Bic to Quebec and return, are $4.60 and $4.15 per foot draft respectively. The pilotage of a vessel of 18 feet draft, towards the close of the season, would therefore be $229.50

It appears from the foregoing pilotage statements, that the disadvantage to Montreal, is very much more one of *distance* than *expense*. The rates are all higher to other ports than to Montreal; and the totals for the summer season compare as follows:—

		Total Mileage.		Pilotage Charges.
To and from Boston................		18	....	$117.90
"	New York,............	42	....	172.80
"	Philadelphia	206	....	162.00
"	Baltimore	354	....	180.00
"	Montreal	622	....	193.50

1. It is suggested that when the system of telegraphic communication in the Gulf and River St. Lawrence is completed, pilotage arrangements may be very much simplified, and the services of Pilots be made more available than heretofore, and their numbers largely reduced. This may be effected by the establishing of a station or stations, with which the masters of in-coming vessels could communicate by use of the electro-signal service.

2. The Pilot-service ought to be an open one,—to which all competent men should be admitted, and each Pilot allowed to receive and hold all his own earnings.

3. No deep-sea pilotage charges should be exacted from any vessel, upward or downward, when in tow of a tug, the Master of which is a duly licensed Pilot of the first-class.

4. Rates of pilotage should be reduced, and all inefficient or incapable men removed from the Pilot rolls.

VI.—THE TOWAGE QUESTION.

6th. What remedy your Board would propose to lessen the cost of Towage of Sailing Vessels from Father Point to Quebec and from Quebec to Montreal.

Although rates of towage at other ocean-ports are not asked for by the MINISTER OF PUBLIC WORKS, it has been considered worth while, as far as practicable, to make a comparison on a basis similar to that on which the information about Pilotage has been given.

1.—PORT OF BOSTON.

The rates for towing a 600-ton vessel, drawing 18 feet water, from Boston Light to dock, and *vice versa*, are :—

Inward,......................	$35.00
Outward,......................	35.00
	$70.00

If a vessel takes a tug outside of Boston Light, inwards,—or is towed outward beyond that Light,—the additional service is a matter of agreement between the vessel and the tug.

2.—PORT OF NEW YORK.

A 600-ton vessel may be towed at the following rates :—

Inward,......................	$35.00
Outward, ...	35.00
	$70.00

Masters of vessels make bargains with tug-boats to tow in accordance with the necessities of the case. Sometimes, wind and tide favoring, the tug leaves the vessel at the Narrows, which is 6 miles from the Battery ;—with wind and tide unfavorable, the tug will go 15 to 20 miles.

"There are no legal rates established for towing, the charge depending on distance, "state of weather, and size of vessel. In favorable weather, a vessel of 300 or 400 tons "can be towed in for $30 ; 600 tons, $35 ; 1000 tons, $45, and if the vessel knows "where she is to be docked, this is included. *If the vessel is, for any reason, obliged to use* "*steam to come in, much higher rates are required.* Outward towage is governed by the "same rules."

3.—PORT OF PHILADELPHIA.

The charges for towing a 600-ton vessel, drawing 18 feet water, from the Capes of the Delaware to the city, a distance of 103 miles, would be :—

> Inward, 50c. per mile $51.50
> Outward, 75c. per mile 77.25
>
> $128.75

Summer rates are by agreement. Inward-bound craft frequently sail up to Reedy Island, which is 46 miles from the city, and there take steam. It is not usual for outward vessels to tow below Reedy Island. In that case the towage would only cost $57.56.

The tug-boats on the Delaware River are said to be the most powerful in the world, being each of about 2,500 horse power.

4.—PORT OF BALTIMORE.

Towage charges on a 600-ton vessel, 18 feet draft of water, from Cape Henry to Baltimore, 177 miles, would be :—

> Inward, ... $142.00
> Outward, ... 142.00
>
> $284.00

5.—PORT OF MONTREAL.

It would be misleading to quote rates of towage here, as in the foregoing examples; for the simple reason that though tow-boat officials sometimes refer to the "regular tariff," there is practically no recognized tariff of rates for tug-boat service in the Gulf and River St. Lawrence. There seems to have been one, however, bearing date 1874; because the Canada Shipping Company framed a list of charges for season 1880, for the services, when required, of their tug "Lake," the terms being mentioned as 50 per cent. less than those of 1874. According to that reduction a 600-ton vessel, drawing 18 feet water, would be charged 46c. per ton for first-class service, from Quebec to Montreal, or $276 for the trip, (the downward rates by both tariffs being 25 per cent. less,) while the charge under the *regime* of 1874 would presumably be $552. But there was in 1876, a towage tariff issued by "Opposition Tow-Boats," according to which the rate for a vessel as above, was 91c. per ton, or $546 up from Quebec. The difference between the supposed-to-be regular tariff of 1874, and the one of 1876, was so small as to lead to the belief that the opposition was of a very nominal kind, —serving only to mislead unsuspecting ship-masters. The above-mentioned Company's rate from Father Point to Quebec is $175, or $306.25 both ways.

6.—How the Towage Business is Worked.

The towing-service in the River and Gulf of St. Lawrence has been characterized as inefficient,—it being alleged that there are steamers of one kind and another engaged in it, that were not originally intended for that sort of work, and which, as might be expected, are poorly adapted for it. The tariff rates charged, too, are exorbitantly high, the mode of exacting them is arbitrary and irregular, often oppressive—it seeming to be the settled belief of tow-boat organizations, that the commerce of Canada's Great Water-Highway *must* afford them revenue.*

A number of detailed lists have been obtained of vessels,—showing tonnage, draft, rates of charge, &c., &c.,—towed for varying distances between Bic and Quebec up to Montreal, and return, in the seasons of navigation 1878, 1879 and 1880;—and they indicate how inconsistent and inequitable are the rates levied. It would unnecessarily swell this answer, to give the lists here-referred-to in full; but the following brief *résumé* of some of them may be sufficiently explicit.

Season of Navigation, 1878.—Out of one list of 24 vessels towed up to Montreal and back to Quebec, the sum exacted in four instances was $550, the tonnages being respectively 803, 349, 690, and 349. Four vessels paid $500 each, the respective tonnages being 744, 699, 739, and 388. Four vessels paid $300 each, the respective tonnages being 633, 398, 490, and 288. A vessel of 633 tons paid $285, and one of 414 tons paid $212.

Season of Navigation, 1879.—Out of one list of 14 vessels, one of 510 tons paid $811.45;—one of 813 tons paid $500;—$450 was paid for one of 729 tons;—$440 for 830 tons;—$425 for 628 tons, and $195 for 521 tons.

Season of Navigation, 1880.—Out of 14 vessels, the amount exacted in two instances was $500 each, the tonnages respectively being 871 and 872. The sum of $450 was paid for 787 tons;—$400 each for 729, 364, and 354;—$350 for 769;—$330 for 396;—$250 for 237;—$230 for 147;—and $225 for 249 tons.

Further for 1880.—A barque of 1000 tons paid $600 for towage from below Quebec to Montreal and return; while a ship of 1135 tons had to pay

---

* A well-informed person at Quebec, writes somewhat roughly, under date 20th September, as follows:—

"The Tariff made by the Beaver Line, is just one-half of that for 1876, but we " don't even get that for four-fifths of the vessels. There have been seven vessels taken up "this year, that have paid full tariff; but that was caused by the ignorance of the Masters, "and the unblushing lying of Agents, which some of the Tug-owners keep for the pur- "pose. Several of us have given orders not to take Montreal vessels at the low rates "current,—but to give Quebec vessels a preference in all cases. The detention of Pilots "up and down, expenses in current, and moorages in harbor, have rendered the business, " at current rates, a losing one."

$1,325. In the latter instance, the Master was on his first trip to the River St. Lawrence; and he imagined the matter was all right when, without stating any sum, the official on the tug said he would be *towed up for 20 per cent. less than the tariff rate !* A barque of 770 tons was charged $250; while another of 500 tons had to pay $810 for like service. A brigantine of 508 tons recently paid $260 from below Quebec to Montreal and return; the same Agents having, in 1879, a barque of 510 tons which had to pay more than three times that amount for similar service. A tug offered to take a vessel up to Montreal and back to Quebec for $450,—to which the Captain assented, on condition that if his Agent at the latter port had made any arrangement, he should not be required to pay more than the Agent had bargained for. On arrival it was found that an agreement had been made for $300.

The vessels which suffer most are those which come into the St. Lawrence trade for the first time; and their experience is often so hard and cheerless that they never return. The greatest perplexity and annoyance experienced by owners of tonnage in Europe are believed to arise mainly from the uncertainty of towage expenses; and there can hardly be a doubt that this keeps away many a ship from Montreal, giving color to the exaggerated reports which have gained credence respecting exorbitant charges of every kind to which all vessels are subjected.

7.—Suggestions towards a Remedy.

1. Rates of towage should be reduced to a minimum, and the Harbor Trust of Montreal might be empowered to provide towage facilities, at not more than cost of service.

2. Or, a Company with suitable vessels, might be subsidised for the purpose of procuring strict adherence to rates *under* cost to vessels.

3. Or, it might be worth considering, whether the service should be left open to competition by all tow-boats that may be *licensed* as to their fitness, and to be governed by a uniform tariff of rates, which shall be maxima. Vessels towed could be left, during the busy season, in Hochelaga Bay, until there is berth-room,—and then brought up by the chain-tug, and docked by a harbor-tug, at fixed rates, which should be deducted from the tow-boats' accounts.

4. The Captain of all tug-boats should be licensed Pilots.

5. For the prevention of any possible over-charge, all rates for towage might be made payable at the Office of the Harbor Trust.

ADDITIONAL INFORMATION.

RATES OF OCEAN FREIGHT.

There is a current theory that the larger the vessel the less the cost of transport. As regards the Upper Lake Trade, the President of the Buffalo Board of Trade has put the case thus:—

" At the same rates a vessel carrying 60,000 Bushels of corn makes a profit of $740 on the round trip from Chicago to Buffalo and return, where a vessel carrying 21,000 bushels gains but $83.30, the rates in this case being 2 cents per bushel for corn and $1.00 per ton for coal (carried on the return trip), giving to each vessel the same proportionate return cargo. Calling the rate 4 cents per bushel for corn and $1.00 per ton for coal, the smaller vessel would gain $743.50 while the larger one would show $2,540 on the profit side of the ledger."

Writing to the Secretary, under date 2nd November, 1874, the late Hon. JOHN YOUNG, then Chairman of the Montreal Harbor Commission, said:—

" The effect on the cost of outward freight, by the deepening of the channel to 20 feet, and employing the large ship, has been to reduce freight 33⅓ per cent., compared with the rates current previous to the improvement of the channel.........The Harbor Commissioners believe that the cost of freight will thus be diminished, and, as a consequence, that the value of what is exported will be increased to the producer, and imports cheapened to the consumer."

Only a day or two before Hon. Mr. YOUNG's decease, he requested that a statement of ocean freight-rates at Montreal should be prepared,—going as far back as the record of the Corn Exchange Association would admit of,—he being of opinion that the quotations would show a continuance of the reduction.

Since then a good deal of labor and care have been expended in arranging a table of average rates of Ocean freight for heavy Grain to Liverpool, by steamships and sailing vessels, for each month and for each year from 1861 to 1879 inclusive,—see next page.

AVERAGE RATES OF FREIGHT FOR HEAVY GRAIN PER 480 LBS. FROM MONTREAL TO LIVERPOOL.

YEAR.	MAY. Sail.	MAY. Steam.	JUNE. Sail.	JUNE. Steam.	JULY. Sail.	JULY. Steam.	AUGUST. Sail.	AUGUST. Steam.	SEPTEMBER. Sail.	SEPTEMBER. Steam.	OCTOBER. Sail.	OCTOBER. Steam.	NOVEMBER. Sail.	NOVEMBER. Steam.	AVERAGE for year. Sail.	AVERAGE for year. Steam.
	s. d.	s. d.	s. d.	s. d.	s. d.	s. d.	s. d.	s. d.	s. d.	s. d.	s. d.	s. d.	s. d.	s. d.	s. d.	s. d.
1861......	8 3	......	7 6	......	7 7½	......	6 1½	......	......	......	8 1½	......	9 6	......	7 10	......
1862......	6 10½	10 0	7 0½	10 0	7 11½	9 2	9 6	9 5	9 0½	10 5	9 9	11 1	9 9	12 5	8 7	10 4
1863......	6 7½	7 11	6 3½	8 0	6 2½	7 10	6 1	6 7½	6 3	5 10½	3 10½	5 2	3 11½	6 4	5 7½	6 10
1864......	5 3	6 3½	6 0	6 9½	5 1	5 5	5 3	5 7	5 6	5 11	4 7½	5 0	......	......	5 3½	5 10
1865	3 9	3 9	3 9	3 9	......	4 11½	......	4 6	......	5 0	4 6	6 1	4 1½	6 0	4 0½	4 10
1866......	......	7 0	5 2½	6 2	4 9	5 0	4 2	4 4½	4 2	4 10	......	5 10	5 0	7 11	4 8	5 10½
1867......	5 1	6 6	4 7	6 6	4 8½	6 1½	......	5 3½	......	6 3	7 10	9 4	8 9	11 10½	6 2	7 5
1868......	4 3	6 10½	4 6	5 7½	......	4 2½	......	4 0	4 9	......	5 6	6 7	5 3	7 0	4 10	5 8½
1869......	3 4½	4 6	6 0	5 3½	......	5 8½	6 1½	5 7½	7 5	7 6½	7 0	8 2	7 0	8 5	6 2	6 5½
1870......	5 5½	5 7½	4 9	6 0½	4 3	4 1½	6 0	6 1	4 10½	5 5	4 8	4 11	4 10½	6 5	5 0	5 6
1871......	5 3	5 10½	6 1	6 10½	5 10½	5 10½	6 7½	6 8½	7 1	7 6½	7 0	8 6	7 1	8 6	6 5	7 1½
1872......	4 4	4 10	5 2	5 2	6 1	6 1	6 0	6 0	6 11	6 11	8 5	9 0½	7 6	7 9	6 4	6 6½
1873......	7 1½	7 1½	8 6	8 11½	7 6	8 9	7 7	8 4	9 10	10 8	......	......	12 6	13 6	8 10	9 7
1874......	8 7	8 11	6 8½	7 3	5 7	6 1	3 9	4 9	4 0	4 1½	3 6	4 6½	4 1½	5 7½	5 3	5 10½
1875	4 7½	4 5½	5 1	5 4½	4 7½	5 5	5 8½	5 8½	5 9	5 2½	7 2	7 2	8 7½	8 7½	5 11	6 0
1876	......	5 6	......	5 8½	......	5 3	4 10½	4 9	5 2½	5 1½	6 1	6 1	5 5	5 5	5 5	5 5
1877......	4 0½	4 0½	4 4	4 4	3 7½	3 7½	4 10	4 10	7 2	7 2	8 2½	8 2½	7 10	7 10	5 8½	5 8½
1878......	5 6	5 6	5 11½	5 11½	5 1	5 1	4 4½	4 4½	4 7	4 7	5 0½	5 2	5 11	5 11	5 2½	5 2¾
1879......	3 5	3 5	3 7	3 7	3 9	3 9	5 4	5 4	5 8¼	5 8¼	No quotations.	7 0	No quotations.	6 6	4 4¼	5 0½

The average annual rates for steam and sail are shown in the last column. Separating these yearly averages into two periods of nine years each,—the first one (1862 to 1870,) gives an average rate of 5s. 7d. Stg. per 480 lbs. for sail-craft, and 6s. 6d. for steamships,—the averages for the second (1871 to 1879,) being respectively 5s. 11d. and 6s. 3d. These results show an increase of 4d. for sail-craft, during the last period, but a *decrease* of 3d. for steamships. It would appear, therefore, that, on the foregoing theory, all the advantages of larger vessels have not yet accrued to Montreal exporters. There can be no doubt, however, that the greater tonnage of the vessels employed in the regular grain-carrying trade of the River St. Lawrence (especially of steamships) in later years. has given facilities for vastly more rapid transportation of larger cargoes.

A remark made elsewhere, regarding freight-rates on inland waters, may be repeated here, viz., that while *averages* for periods of years are *convenient* criteria, they do not always afford sufficient data for conclusions. The tables on pp. 35 and 36, will enable the enquirer to ascertain the rates of ocean-freights on one day in each week during the seasons of summer navigation in 1878 and 1879, at Montreal, Boston, New York and Baltimore; while a table on page 37 affords data for comparing rates once a week at New York and Montreal, in the present year (1880).

Comparative Rates from Montreal and Boston to Liverpool for two years.

DATE.	1878. MONTREAL TO LIVERPOOL. Per 480 lbs. SAIL.	1878. MONTREAL TO LIVERPOOL. Per 480 lbs. STEAM.	BOSTON to LIVERPOOL p. 60 lbs. STEAM.	1879. MONTREAL TO LIVERPOOL. Per 480 lbs. SAIL.	1879. MONTREAL TO LIVERPOOL. Per 480 lbs. STEAM.	BOSTON to LIVERPOOL p. 60 lbs. STEAM.
	s. d. s. d.	s. d. s. d.	d.	s. d. s. d.	s. d. s. d.	d.
Jan. 3	....@	9 0/@	8½	...@	8 0 @	....
" 10	"	"	9	"	8 0 "	5
" 17	"	"	9	"	6 6 "	5
" 24	"	"	9	"	6 6 "	5½
" 31	"	"	10	"	6 6 "	5¼
Feb. 7	"	"	10	"	6 6 "	5½
" 14	"	"	10	"	6 6 "	5½
" 21	"	"	9	"	6 6 "	5½
" 28	Navigation Closed. "	Navigation Closed. "	9	"	6 6 "	5½
March 7	"	"	8	"	6 6 "	5½
" 14	"	"	7	"	6 6 "	6
" 21	"	"	7	"	6 6 "	6
" 28	"	"	6	"	6 6 "	5¼
April 4	"	"	7	"	6 6 "	5¼
" 11	"	"	6½	"	6 6 "	5½
" 18	"	"	7	"	.... "	5¼
" 25	"	"	6½	"	4 6 " 4 9	5
May 2	"	"	6¾	"	3 6 " 4 0	5
" 9	5 0 " 5 6	5 0 " 5 6	7	"	3 6 " 4 0	5
" 16	5 3 " 5 9	5 3 " 5 9	7	3 3 " 4 0	3 3 " 4 0	5
" 23	5 3 " 5 9	5 3 " 5 9	7	2 6 " 3 6	2 6 " 3 6	5
" 30	.... "	5 6 " 6 0	7	.... "	2 6 " 4 0	5
June 6	5 9 " 6 0	5 9 " 6 0	6¾	2 9 " 4 0	2 9 " 4 0	5
" 13	5 9 " 6 0	5 9 " 6 0	6¾	2 9 " 4 0	2 9 " 4 0	5
" 20	.... "	6 0 " 6 3	6¾	3 3 " 4 3	3 3 " 4 3	5
" 27	.... "	5 9 " 6 3	6¾	3 3 " 4 3	3 3 " 4 3	4
July 4	.... "	5 6 " 6 0	6¾	3 0 " 4 3	3 0 " 4 3	4
" 11	.... "	4 6 " 5 9	6½	2 9 " 4 0	2 9 " 4 0	3
" 18	4 6 " 5 0	4 6 " 5 0	6½	3 0 " 4 3	3 0 " 4 3	6
" 25	4 6 " 5 0	4 6 " 5 0	6½	3 9 " 5 0	3 9 " 5 0	7
Aug. 1	4 0 " 4 6	4 0 " 4 6	6½	5 0 " 5 9	5 0 " 5 9	8
" 8	4 0 " 5 0	4 0 " 5 0	6½	5 0 " 6 0	5 0 " 6 0	8
" 15	4 0 " 4 6	4 0 " 4 6	6½	5 0 " 6 0	5 0 " 6 0	8
" 22	4 0 " 4 6	4 0 " 4 6	6½	5 0 " 6 0	5 0 " 6 0	7
" 29	4 3 " 5 0	4 3 " 5 0	6½	4 6 " 5 0	4 6 " 5 0	7
Sept. 5	4 6 " 5 0	4 6 " 5 0	6½	5 0 " 5 9	5 0 " 5 9	6
" 12	4 6 " 5 0	4 6 " 5 0	6½	5 3 " 6 0	5 3 " 6 0	6
" 19	4 0 " 5 0	.... "	6	5 3 " 6 0	5 3 " 6 0	7
" 26	4 3 " 4 6	4 3 " 4 6	6	5 9 " 6 6	5 9 " 6 6	7½
Oct. 3	5 0 " 5 3	5 0 " 5 3	6	.... "	6 0 " 6 6	7½
" 10	.... "	5 0 " 5 3	6	.... "	6 0 " 7 6	8½
" 17	.... "	5 0 " 5 3	6	.... "	7 0 " 7 6	9
" 24	4 6 " 5 0	5 0 " 5 6	7	.... "	7 6 " 8 0	8½
" 31	5 0 " 5 6	5 0 " 5 6	7½	.... "	6 6 " 7 6	8
Nov. 7	5 6 " 6 0	5 6 " 6 0	8	.... "	6 6 " 7 0	8
" 14	6 6 " 7 0	6 6 " 7 0	7½	.... "	6 0 " 6 6	7
" 21	.... "	.... "	7	"	6 0 " 6 6	6
" 28	"	"	7	"	6 0 " 8 6	6
Dec. 5	Navigation Closed. "	Navigation Closed. "	7	"	6 0 " 8 6	6
" 12	"	"	7	"	6 0 " 7 6	6
" 19	"	"	6	"	6 0 " 7 0	4½
" 26	"	"	5¾	"	6 0 " 7 0	5

Comparative Rates from New York and Baltimore to Liverpool for two years.

Date.		1878. New York to Liverpool. Per 60 lbs. Steam. d.	1878. New York to Liverpool. Per 60 lbs. Sail. d.	1878. Baltimore to Liverpool. Per 60 lbs. Steam. d. @ d.	1879. New York to Liverpool. Per 60 lbs. Steam. d.	1879. New York to Liverpool. Per 60 lbs. Sail. d.	1879. Baltimore to Liverpool. Per 60 lbs. Steam. d.
January	3	9½	8½	11 @ 11½	5¼	....	6
"	10	10	8¼	10¾ @ 11	6	....	6½
"	17	9½	8	11 @ 11½	5¾	....	6½
"	24	9½	7¾	11 @ 11¼	6¼	6	7
"	31	9½	7½	11	5¾	6	7½
February	7	9½	7½	11	5¾	5¼	8
"	14	10	7½	11	6	5	6¾
"	21	9	7¼	11	6	5½	6¾ @ 7
"	28	8	7½	10½ @ 11	6	5½	7¼
March	7	7½	7	10 @ 10½	6¼	5½	7½
"	14	6¾	6½	9½	6½	5¾	7½
"	21	6¾	6½	9 @ 9¼	6	5½	7½
"	28	7	6½	9 @ 9¼	5¾	5¾	6¾ @ 7
April	4	8¼	7½	9	5¾	5¾	6¾
"	11	8	7	8½	6	5¾	7⅛ @ 7¼
"	18	7	6½	8¼ @ 8½	6	5¾	7 @ 7⅛
"	25	7½	7	8½	6¼	5½	6¾
May	2	8½	8	9	5½	5⅜	6¼
"	9	8	7	9¼ @ 9½	5¼	5⅜	6¼ @ 6½
"	16	8	7	8¾ @ 9	5¼	5	6¼ @ 6½
"	23	7¾	6½	8 @ 8½	5⅛	5	6
"	30	8	7	8	5¼	5	5
June	6	8¼	7	8½	5¼	5	5
"	13	8¼	7	8¾ @ 9	5	4¼	4½ @ 5
"	20	8¼	7¼	9	4¾	4¼	6 asked
"	27	7¾	7¼	8¾ @ 9	4¼	4¼	4 @ 4½
July	4	7	....	8½ @ 8¾	4	4¼	4 @ 4½
"	11	7	....	8¼ @ 8½	5	4¼	5
"	18	6¾	....	7	6½	....	7 @ 7½
"	25	6	5	8	7½	....	7½ @ 8
August	1	7¾	6	8	7¾	....	8¼ @ 8¾
"	8	8	6	8	8½	....	8¼ @ 8¾
"	15	8	....	7½ @ 8	7½	7½ @ 8	8 @ 8½
"	22	7½	7	7½	7¾	7	8
"	29	7	7	7½ @ 8	7¾	7	7¾ @ 8
September	5	6¼	....	7½	7	....	7½
"	12	5½	....	6½ @ 7	6½	....	6½ @ 6¾
"	19	5½	....	6¼ @ 6½	7¾	7	6½ @ 6¾
"	26	6¼	....	6¼	7¾	....	7 @ 8
October	3	6½	6	6½	9	9	9
"	10	6½	6½	6 @ 6½	9	9	9
"	17	7½	....	8	8½	8	9¼
"	24	7½	....	8	7¾	7½	8½
"	31	8	7½	8	6¾	6½	9
November	7	7¾	7¾	8½	8	7	9
"	14	7½	7½	8⅝ @ 8¾	6½	7	9 @ 9¼
"	21	7¾	7½	8½ @ 8¾	6¼	7	7 asked
"	28	7¾	7½	8½	6¼	6	6 @ 6¼
December	5	7¼	7¼	7¾ @ 8	5¼	5	5
"	12	6	....	8¼	4	4½	4
"	19	5½	....	7½	4	4½	5
"	26	5¾	....	7 @ 7½	3	....	5

The following quotations for 1880, show rates in Montreal as compared with New York:—

DATE.	MONTREAL.					NEW YORK.	
1880.	PER QUARTER OF 480 LBS. Iron Clipper and Steam.			PER BUSH. OF 60 LBS. Iron Clipper and Steam.		PER BUSH. OF 60 LBS. Steam.	Sail.
	$s.$ $d.$		$s.$ $d.$	$d.$	$d.$	$d.$	$d.$
May 7......	4 0	@	4 6 =	6 @	$6\frac{3}{4}$	$4\frac{1}{2}$	$4\frac{1}{2}$
" 14......	3 9	"	4 3 =	$5\frac{5}{8}$ "	$6\frac{3}{4}$	$4\frac{1}{2}$	$4\frac{1}{4}$
" 21......	3 9	"	4 3 =	$5\frac{3}{5}$ "	$6\frac{5}{8}$	5	$3\frac{1}{2}$ @ 4
28......	3 6	"	4 0 =	$5\frac{1}{4}$ "	6	3	....
June 4......	3 6		4 0 =	$5\frac{1}{4}$ "	6	4	3 @ $3\frac{1}{2}$
" 11......	3 9	"	4 3 =	$5\frac{5}{8}$ "	$6\frac{3}{8}$	5	$3\frac{1}{2}$
" 18......	4 0	"	4 3 =	6 "	$6\frac{3}{4}$	5 @ $5\frac{1}{4}$	$4\frac{1}{4}$
" 25......	4 3	"	5 0 =	$6\frac{3}{8}$ "	$7\frac{1}{2}$	6	$4\frac{1}{2}$ @ 5
July 2......	4 9	"	5 3 =	$7\frac{3}{4}$ "	$7\frac{7}{8}$	....	....
" 9......	4 9	"	5 6 =	$7\frac{1}{8}$ "	$8\frac{1}{4}$	6 @ $6\frac{1}{2}$	5
" 16......	4 6	"	5 6 =	$6\frac{3}{4}$ "	$8\frac{1}{4}$	$6\frac{1}{2}$	$6\frac{1}{2}$
" 23......	5 0	"	5 6 =	$7\frac{1}{2}$ "	$8\frac{1}{4}$	8	$6\frac{1}{2}$
30......	5 3	"	6 0 =	$7\frac{7}{8}$ "	9	9 @ $9\frac{1}{4}$	$7\frac{1}{2}$
August 6......	5 6	"	6 0 =	$8\frac{1}{4}$	9	8	$7\frac{1}{2}$
" 13......	5 0	"	5 9 =	$7\frac{1}{2}$ "	$8\frac{5}{8}$	$7\frac{1}{4}$	....
" 20......	4 0	"	5 0 =	6 "	$7\frac{1}{2}$	$6\frac{1}{2}$	....
" 27......	3 6	"	4 3 =	$5\frac{1}{4}$ "	$6\frac{3}{8}$	$6\frac{1}{4}$	....
Sept. 3......	3 0	"	4 0 =	$4\frac{1}{2}$ "	6	$6\frac{1}{4}$	....
" 10......	2 9	"	3 6 =	$4\frac{5}{8}$ "	$5\frac{1}{4}$	$5\frac{1}{4}$	....
" 17......	2 9	"	3 6 =	$4\frac{1}{8}$ "	$5\frac{1}{4}$	$5\frac{1}{4}$	....
" 24......	2 9	"	3 9 =	$4\frac{1}{8}$ "	$5\frac{5}{8}$	$5\frac{1}{4}$ @ $5\frac{1}{2}$	....
Oct. 1......	3 3	"	4 0 =	$4\frac{7}{8}$ "	6	$5\frac{1}{2}$ @ $5\frac{3}{4}$	....
" 8......	4 0	"	5 0 =	6 "	$7\frac{1}{2}$	$6\frac{1}{4}$	....
" 15......	4 0		5 0 =	6 "	$7\frac{1}{2}$	6	....

There is a consideration that must not be overlooked, viz: that, other things being equal, the prevalence of high rates of ocean freight might be expected to induce vessels to seek the port where these can be obtained. A fair axiom would be:—High rates of freight, *cet. par.*, should bring tonnage to the St. Lawrence,—more vessels would, by competition, tend to lower rates,—and this cheapening of transportation would naturally bring more freight to Montreal. The question is, therefore, a pertinent one:—What has prevented more vessels from seeking the port where they could seemingly earn most money?—and the reply is,—nothing but the more than countervailing charges that would be incurred. The hoped-for advantages of lower rates of freight, will be the result of lower port dues, less exorbitant towage charges, cheaper pilotage, and such improvements for navigating the River and Gulf as will lead to lower rates of insurance.

But notwithstanding all the drawbacks and disadvantages, there are, this year, two features in the trade of the River St. Lawrence, deserving of notice. (1.) There has been a steady flow of Grain from the West for shipment across the Atlantic on other than Montreal account; and (2.) steam tonnage seeking charter, appears to be beginning to prefer Montreal over other Atlantic ports when offering rates are the same. As before suggested, this is, no doubt, to be attributed to the increased depth of water in the ship-channel, as well as to the agitation about reduction of dues and other charges.

CRAFT FOR PORTS OF CALL.

It is worthy of note that, while the charges incident to the deepening of the ship-channel bear heavily upon tonnage and merchandise, this is measurably compensated for by the much larger class of steam and sail vessels now engaged in the *regular* trade between Montreal and Great Britain; for it seems that increased carrying capacity has not, within the past fifteen or twenty years, further resulted in materially lessening freight-rates. But there is another class of serviceable vessels, of much smaller tonnage, (say 400 to 700 tons,) and that with a full cargo, draw from 15 to 18 or 19 feet of water, which it is considered desirable to keep in the St. Lawrence trade. It is alleged on behalf of such craft, hailing from Norway, Sweden, Germany, Austria, Italy, Spain, &c., that the improvement of the ship-channel to any depth beyond 20 feet, involves an inequitable per centage of assessment on them. The pilotage and harbor charges, and especially the uncertain and arbitrary rates often levied for towage, have tended to drive them away. The table on page 39 shows the number and tonnages of vessels (steam and sail) which came to the port of Montreal during the past decade, and cleared with Grain to ports of call "for orders."

The decrease of vessels and cargoes in 1879 is remarkable, and unless the shipments formerly "for orders" are now being made direct to Continental Ports, it may be fairly inferred that shippers of Grain have so far lost some advantage which they formerly had when they used the class of vessels here referred to. The enlarged capacity of steam and sail vessels in the regular trade, and the constantly increasing per centage of steam tonnage, do not entirely compensate for their absence. From the statements on pp. 29, 30, 31 about towage, it will

YEAR	No. OF VESSELS			TONNAGE			CARGOES						
	STEAM	SAIL	TOTAL	STEAM	SAIL	TOTAL	WHEAT	CORN	PEAS	OATS	BARLEY & RYE	FLOUR	TOTAL
							Bushels.	Bushels.	Bushels.	Bushels.	Bushels.	Barrels.	Bushels.
1870	....	....	26	......	......	9,835	306,395	....	16,000	....	....	1,600	330,395
1871	....	....	74	......	......	27,203	408,463	22,376	....	....	....	....	430,839
1872	14	66	80	11,653	25,136	36,789	363,810	1,791,126	15,000	....	....	....	2,169,936
1873	18	56	74	14,305	20,413	34,718	1,561,133	556,734	29,338	....	....	3,519	2,164,800
1874	21	75	96	17,018	31,301	48,319	1,727,864	716,778	180,169	35,207	....	1,000	2,665,018
1875	1	93	94	955	37,474	38,429	1,659,233	241,699	261,063	....	....	....	2,161,995
1876	2	90	92	2,117	35,491	37,608	738,084	1,122,793	156,837	102,437	....	1,284	2,126,571
1877	26	60	86	21,474	27,862	49,336	1,243,155	971,724	208,211	24,360	445,317	....	2,892,767
1878	12	77	89	11,502	34,803	46,305	1,210,880	958,698	383,088	17,747	47,380	....	2,617,793
1879	....	54	54	......	24,132	24,132	725,161	319,500	291,900	....	17,901	....	1,354,462

be seen how heavily and arbitrarily the charges for that service, bear upon the class of vessels which have heretofore been in favor for ports of call.

There is another view of this part of the subject, as regards the trade of Montreal, which is very seldom taken into account,—viz., the loss that would be sustained by tradesmen and dealers, if the vessels here referred to are compelled to forsake the St. Lawrence. It may be stated, on the authority of firms doing business in this city, that, exclusively of pilotage, towage, harbor dues, &c., the average disbursements of vessels of 600 to 1000 tons register, is about $800 each. If this be so, then the absence of 35 port-of-call vessels in 1879, (that being the difference as compared with 1878), involved a loss to the local trade of $28,000.

RATES OF MARINE INSURANCE.

The question of Marine Insurance is one of considerable importance in relation to the trade of the River and Gulf of St. Lawrence—rates heretofore having often constituted a considerable charge both upon imports and exports, and sometimes without equitable discrimination as to risk. The following are comparative (*nominal*) rates at the ports of New York and Montreal :—

| | NEW YORK. | | MONTREAL. | |
	SAIL.	STEAM.	SAIL.	STEAM.
	per cent.	per cent.	per cent.	per cent.
To London	¾ @ 2½	¼ @ 1	¾ @ 3	½ @ 1½
Liverpool	¾ " 2½	¼ " 1	¾ " 3	½ " 1½
Glasgow	¾ " 2½	⅜ " 1	¾ " 3	½ " 1½
Cork	¾ " 2½	½ " 1	¾ " 3	⅝ " 1½
Havre	¾ " 2½	¼ " 1	¾ " 3	¾ " 1½
Hamburg) Bremen (	¾ " 2½	⅜ " 1½	¾ " 3	¾ " 1½
Bordeaux	1 " 2	½ " 1	1 " 3½	1 " 2
Smyrna) Trieste (	1½ " 2	¾ " 1¼		....

The rates thus formulated would be apt to mislead, without a word or two of explanation; for, even if the quotations were uniformly obtained, there is a deduction of 20 per cent. made at both ports by American Companies, and 10 per cent. by European ones, the rates of the latter being said to be lower. Both of the statements give a wide range for the season. At Montreal, before the 1st of September, risks have been taken this year on grain in A 1 steam tonnage at ⅜ths per cent., and at ½ to ¾ths per cent. by iron clippers and steamers in the regular trade. There is a rule,—not exactly an iron-clad one,—by which there is a rise in rates of ⅛th per cent. on and after 1st September, and further similar advances on 15th September, 1st October, and 15th October respectively. Each addition of ⅛th per cent. is equal to $1 on every 1,000 bushels of wheat so insured; the increase of ½ per cent. within the six weeks would, therefore, be equal to $4 on every 1,000 bushels of wheat, and would add more than $7,000 to the cost of the quantity (about 1,785,000 bushels) shipped from Montreal from 1st September to 20th October, in the present year. It is said that the ratio of advance on and after 15th October depends upon the weather; this therefore, involves a special arrangement.

The rates tabulated above are somewhat higher for Montreal risks, than for those of New York. It has been remarked, however, that insurances have been effected on some occasions lately in which the difference favored shippers here; and Insurance Companies appear now to be tacitly acknowledging the lessened risk by the competition which exists at variable rates, and below what may be called tariff charges. To say the least of it, there seems to be no good reason now for the same Companies exacting higher premiums on grain cargoes, for instance, shipped from Montreal, than are accepted by them from New York; for, during a period of seven years, (1873 to 1879 inclusive), of all the shipments from Montreal under the Port Warden's regulations,—*not a single accident or loss occurred all that time, in consequence of a vessel being grain-laden.* On the other hand, during a period of about nine months, (1st September, 1878, to 11th June, 1879), of the vessels which loaded grain at New York, seven (7) were abandoned, and thirteen (13) reported missing.

The arrangements which have been in progress during the past three years, at the instance of the Dominion Government, for extending the telegraphic system to the principal islands of the Gulf,—notably, Anticosti, the Magdalen and St. Paul's Islands, Bird Rocks, &c., are now on the eve of completion. The light-houses in the River and Gulf of St. Lawrence will be placed in telegraphic connection with the shore-lines and signal stations, to work in accord with the International Code, which is capable of indicating 78,642 distinct signals. The project includes the establishment of a daily *Telegraphic Bulletin*, for transmitting frequent reports about the weather, vessels passing inward or outward, casualties, and communicating with pilot stations, tug companies, &c. When the work is completed,—as it will probably be about the opening of navigation in 1881,—it will be easy and safe for ships to navigate the great Canadian Water Highway. This surely warrants a considerable reduction in rates of marine insurance, and a large increase in the steam and sail fleet in the trade of the St. Lawrence.

SUMMARY OF CONCLUSIONS.

1. The carrying trade of Canada, via the River St. Lawrence, is embarrassed by a multitude of charges and rates of one kind and another; some are large, while many, singly and apart from the others, erroneously appear to persons unacquainted with details, to be of very little consequence. Water-borne merchandise from and to the West by the St. Lawrence route should be relieved from every extraneous burden,—otherwise, our fair share of West-bound traffic, and the proportionate volume of the eastward traffic will continue to decrease. Such an untoward result would make it appear that the many millions of dollars invested in the Canals and Ship-Channel have been expended in vain. It seems, therefore, to be the dictate of wisdom that *the water-highways of the Dominion should, in the meantime, be made available for enlarging and extending Canadian commerce, whether they yield any present direct revenue to the Government or not.*

2. MONTREAL CAN BE MADE THE CHEAPEST AND BEST PORT IN THE WORLD, for sea-going steam and sail tonnage. Such a consummation would be of incalculable benefit to the trade and commerce of the whole country ; and the hearty co-operation of the Shipping Interest and the Commercial Organizations, with the Harbor Trust, the Civic Authorities, and the Dominion Government, is invoked for its accomplishment.

3. The Dominion Government should immediately relieve the Harbor Trust from the expense attending the deepening of Lake St. Peter, and improving the Ship-Channel between Montreal and Quebec.

4. Wharfage on all ocean-cargoes, inward and outward, should be reduced to the lowest possible rates, or if practicable abolished. Wharfage on ocean-tonnage should be reduced to the level of Baltimore and Philadelphia, and abolished on grain-carrying inland craft.

5. Canal tolls on Breadstuffs and Provisions should be abolished, and inland traffic should be exempted from all obstructive charges. The use of the electric light in the harbor of Montreal, now admits of loading and unloading at night,—to prevent detentions, therefore, between Kingston and Montreal, it

will be essential to have Lakes St. Louis and St. Francis lighted, so as to be navigable by night for tows of barges.

6.   The Harbor Trust of Montreal ought to be authorized to provide for an efficient towage service, at lowest possible rates.

7.   With a view to greater efficiency, and to provide for the anticipated increase of vessels coming into the St. Lawrence trade, the Pilotage service should be remodelled, and pilotage charges reduced.

8.   Rates and charges incident to the transfer, storage, and loading of Grain cargoes should be reduced to a minimum.

9.   An effort should be made to reduce rates of premium of ocean marine insurance in accordance with lessened risks secured by the Port Warden's service, and the electro-signal and telegraphic system in the Gulf and River St. Lawrence.